OVERCOME THE OBSTACLES IN LIFE THAT IMPEDE YOUR GROWTH IN GOD

When You've Had Enough

A Word On Breaking Free

Antoine D. Jackson

Foreword by Pastor Waverly B. Bumbrey, Sr.

Sow Graphics & Publications ~ Southfield, MI 48034

WHEN YOU'VE HAD ENOUGH

Published by Antoine D. Jackson

Southfield, Michigan 48034

All scripture quotations are taken from the King James Version of the Bible, unless otherwise noted.
Copyright © 1977, 1984, 2991 by Thomas Nelson, Inc. and from *The Message*. Copyright © 1993, 1994, 1995, 1996, 2000, 2001, 2002. Used by permission of NavPress Publishing Group

Copyright © 2011 by Antoine D. Jackson ⊙ First Printing

International Standard Book Number 13: 978-1456550240

International Standard Book Number 10: 1456550241

Cover & Interior Design: **SOW Graphics & Publications**

Contributing Designer: Dee Gaymon of **Ktisis Graphic Design**

Edited by Tenita C. Johnson of **So It Is Written, LLC.**

Printed in the United States of America

ALL RIGHTS RESERVED

No part of the publication may be reproduced, stored in a retrieval system, or transmitted, in any form or by any means-electronic, mechanical, photocopying, recording or otherwise- without prior written permission.

This book is dedicated to my beloved grandmother, Mrs. Marie Rosco (1926-2009); your legacy and ministry of love will continue to live on through the many lives you touched as you walked the face of this earth. Take your rest and I love you.

Acknowledgements

I am thankful for the support and words of encouragement of both family and friends through the completion of this project. There are many who assisted me throughout this process to bring this project to culmination.

I offer praise and thanksgiving to my Lord and Savior Jesus Christ. I thankfully express my gratitude for your faithfulness to this man servant. With my lips and my pen, I give all praise unto you Lord for choosing me for this work and for this time. Thank you for providing every one of my needs according to your riches in *Glory through Christ Jesus*. Lord I thank you from the bottom of my heart.

I am deeply grateful for the love and support of my beautiful wife, Joanna Jackson; thank you baby, for allowing me to leave your side in the late hours of the night to commune with God as He spoke the words to me to share in this project. I thank you for your prayers, support, encouragement, recommendations, laughter, snacks, and your listening ear. Thank you for allowing me to be transparent about our lives that our testimony might help others. Your support and dedication to the Lord, first and foremost, means the world to me, and knowing that you stand with me throughout my ministry endeavors causes my heart to fill with joy.

To my daughter, Madison; I thank God for the blessing of your life. My prayer is that your mother and I continue to be Godly examples to you as you grow in the fear and admonition of the Lord.

To my mother Creola and brother Jeffrey. I love you both so much. God blessed me with two of the greatest relatives in the both of you. Despite your illnesses, which were no fought of your own, you both have shown me the greatest amount of love you can show. I pray that while in my care you both feel honored and appreciated.

To my Pastor Waverly B. Bumbrey Sr. and First Lady Patricia A. Bumbrey of Refuge Temple COGIC; your prayers of support and words of encouragement are greatly appreciated. Thank you for your knowledge of the Word and your Godly lifestyles. Your outstanding leadership makes it easy to sit under your tutelage and show respect to your gifts.

To my aunt Articjine Hogan; you introduced me to Christ at an early age, and I am forever grateful for that introduction. To my family and inner circle; your late night conversations and prayers are greatly appreciated.

Ms. Dara T. Munson, President & CEO and my fellow coworkers at Big Brothers Big Sisters of Metropolitan Detroit; thank you for allowing me to minister through my employment.

Rev. Dr. Dwayne Gary, Pastor of Saunders Memorial A.M.E.; your prayers and encouraging words mean so much to me; Ashley "Shon" Wade you are an awesome person and a great organist.

To Stephen and Lynette Simmons; your friendship and prayers are felt daily and your words of encouragement provided strength to keep the faith. Minister Allen and LaKisha Black; you both mean the world to Joanna and I. Lance and LaQuesha Muller, my brother and sister in the faith; you kept saying go ahead and I finally did it. Thank you both for the love you show my wife and I each and every day.

Thanks to you all. I sincerely love you all. I pray God's richest blessings upon you all and hope that our connections in this life prove healthy and effective for us all. Now it's done! I'll be starting the next one tomorrow. ☺

Table of Contents

Acknowledgements

Foreword

Chapter 1 – Profiling the Assailant 15

Chapter 2 – Consider the Source 21

Chapter 3 – A Struggle Over Love 29

Chapter 4 – A Place Called Rehoboth 37

Chapter 5 – Help! I've fallen. Can I Get Up? 47

Chapter 6 – You Don't Qualify 58

Chapter 7 – The Stage of Concretization 65

Chapter 8 – Five Pillars to Secure Victory 70

Chapter 9 – A Final Word On Enough 87

About the Author

Prayer of Salvation

Foreword

Welcome to Antoine Jackson's debut release titled "*When You've Had Enough*." In this book you will discover how to find **victory** over any and all **obstacle**s in your *LIFE*. In this life-changing book, Antoine Jackson uses transparency as his tool to help others be free from Satan's tactics. His audacity to reveal the depths of his life gives us a glimpse of the anointing and the hand of God that rest upon him. He reminds us that Jesus is the *Way, Truth, and the Life* which helps us reach our divine Call in Christ Jesus.

This book will challenge your faith, *because faith that cannot be tested cannot be trusted*. God tries our faith, not to destroy it, but to develop it. In II Thessalonians 1:3, Paul prayed that the suffering Christians in Thessalonica might grow in their faith and God answered his prayers. Antoine's testimonies of real LIFE challenges are written to build the believer's faith that will lead to a victorious life in Christ. The question is: *When Is ENOUGH.....ENOUGH?* It's up to you to decide. The best way to overcome life's challenges is to confront them. Learn how to do that and much more in order to reach your potential in this revealing book, **When You've Had Enough.**

Pastor Waverly B. Bumbrey, BA, MA
Senior Pastor/ Founder, Refuge Temple Church
Detroit, Michigan

A Message from the Author

As you read through the pages of this book, you will hear me talk candidly and truthfully about the struggles that I endured being a caregiver for my mentally impaired mother and brother. Allow me to be straight forward in saying that, I love both my mother and brother and I recognize that their conditions are of no fought of their own. Furthermore, I am in no way attempting to bash them or others who suffer a mental impairment. I am only sharing with you how my natural situation had spiritual implications. It is my hope that you find within my transparency an ability to see how your own natural situations can produce spiritual implications. My natural situations created an environment conducive for Satan to attack, but this book serves as proof that God is able to change you, even when your situation does not change.

Antoine D. Jackson

Chapter 1

PROFILING THE ASSAILANT

As I studied John's gospel, it became clear to me that his writing is more reflective as opposed to the descriptive nature of other gospels. For example, the writer presented the "logos" (the alive Word of God) in an agreeable appearance.

The textual basis that the Lord provided me for this literary work comes from John chapter 8. It is of the essence that before we dive into the lies posed by the enemy that we seek to understand the premise of Jesus' words in John 8:44. Furthermore, it is important to consider the confines, prose, setting, and associations presented in the text that we may be able to properly exegete the scriptures in a productive, efficient, and effective manner.

The gospel of John is the fourth of the synoptic gospels. John's gospel is written in a completely different temperament than that of the other gospels. John's gospel is penned with immense detail that allows the reader to step into the pages and travel back in time. John's gospel reads sort of like a great novel filled with suspense, imagery, plots, themes, and massive amounts of symbolism.

John's gospel takes the reader on a new course not traveled by the other gospel writers. The writer refrains from making mention of stories, information, and in some cases, names used in the other gospels. The writer of John starts off by establishing numerous themes and enrichments, seemingly in an attempt to grab hold of the reader's attention. In the first chapter of John, the writer makes known the identity of Christ. The writer identifies Christ as the incarnate or "alive" Word of God whose charge is to reveal the Father to the world.

The gospel of John is written to the Greek citizens who became Christians during the beginning of the second century. The recipients of this writing were what we might call today "upper class citizens." These individuals were wealthy and educated. However, they possessed a degree of hostility toward a group of displaced people who lived in their towns and who gained deference from the government officials in the city of Rome.

As I studied John's gospel, it became clear to me that his writing is more reflective as opposed to the descriptive nature of other gospels. For example, the writer presented the "logos" (the alive Word of God) in an agreeable appearance. On the contrary, Matthew, Mark, and Luke continued in presenting Jesus as the Jewish Messiah. In addition, they presented Christ as a relative of David and finally, as the eschatological messenger of the end of the world. John, however, removes the legalism found occasionally in the other gospels. For example, he does not include the genealogical history as found in the gospel of Matthew (Matthew 1:1-17), nor does the writer include the Davidic descent as found in the gospel of Luke (Luke 2:4).

Approaching the eighth chapter of John, we find Jesus' objectivity to the crowds gathered. The beginning of the eighth chapter tells us that Jesus went unto the Mount of Olives and early in the morning, he came again in the temple (John 8:1-2) where he sat and taught the people. The text goes on to say that the Scribes and Pharisees brought to him a woman who had been caught in the act of adultery. (John 8:3) We find from Old Testament study that Leviticus Law required that both parties, male and female, be stoned for the sin of adultery. (Leviticus 20:10; Deuteronomy 22:22) However, in anticipation of trapping Jesus in what we might call today a "theological debate", the leaders only brought the woman. The woman's accusers presumably hoped Jesus would say that the woman should not be stoned so that they then could accuse Him of not following

Profiling the Assailant

the laws of Moses. Even more, perhaps they hoped that He *would* agree to stone her. They would then report Him to the Romans because those displaced citizens of the region were not allowed to carry out their own punishments or executions. Jesus, however, knowing the thoughts and intent of the crowd through wisdom, saved the woman's life.

As the text evolves we see time and again where this same group would craft attempts to confuse Jesus or cause Him to indict Himself that they might do away with Him. Nearing the close of the eighth chapter of John, we see again that this off-putting group attempts to trip Jesus up in His words. The writer records when Jesus begins speaking to the group of people who believed on Him saying, *If ye continue in my Word, then are ye my disciples indeed.* (John 8:31) However, standing around was another group seeking to somehow catch Jesus in a bind. Their responses showed their ignorance to the words that Jesus spoke. I imagine that Jesus grew tired of their interruptions and therefore, we find his response recorded in John 8:44.

Ye are of your father the devil, and the lusts of your father ye will do. He was a murderer from the beginning, and abode not in the truth, because there is no truth in him. When he speaketh a lie, he speaketh of his own: for he is a liar, and the father of it.

~John 8:44

Chapter 2

CONSIDER THE SOURCE

The Modi Operandi is the modes of operation used by the devil in an attempt to separate the believer from God's divine purpose for their life. Jesus, in John 8:44 and John 10:10, identifies the modes of operation utilized by the enemy.

Our world is full of information. At times, it is hard to decipher which information is accurate and which is inaccurate. We can go to the local library and check out books on a variety of topics, from adolescent behavior to the zygomatic process. However, to ensure the accuracy of the information, we must always consider the source.

In our text, we find Jesus presenting information to the people who believed in Him. However, gathered around also were those who opposed his teachings and his ministry. Imagine that Jesus is sitting in the synagogue with a group of believers teaching the Word. He has everyone's attention and his message is a "rhema Word" -an on time word for those people's lives; however, somewhere in the back is an unruly parishioner trying to disrupt the service. Jesus, being omniscient or all knowing, can discern their thoughts and hearts. After a while of their ruckus, Jesus grew tired of their interruptions and decides to confront them with information.

There are countless businesses, agencies, institutions, and firms that rely on information to make their products and services come to fruition. Some businesses also employ information as a means of building a case. The United States Federal Bureau of Investigation, better known as the FBI, has a

Consider the Source

special team of investigators known as profilers whose primary task is to extrapolate information about a person, place, or thing based on known traits or tendencies.

Merriam-Webster's Collegiate Dictionary, Eleventh Edition, defines profiling as: *the act of suspecting or targeting a person on the basis of observed characteristics or behavior.* Jesus, after determining enough was enough, decided to confront the group gathered around which was causing havoc. Jesus begins his opening statement by telling those troublemakers gathered around him, *Ye are of your father the devil.* Based on our definition of profiling, it is clear that for Jesus to have made such a blunt and ostensibly controversial statement, He must have first-hand knowledge of the devil.

In the opening chapter of this gospel, the writer gives verification of Jesus' existence, even at the beginning of time, and we know from the Old Testament book of Genesis that Satan existed in the beginning. Additional research discovers that Jesus is recorded in Luke 10:18 saying, *I beheld Satan as lightning fall from heaven.* According to scripture, Jesus knew Satan from day one and having prior knowledge of Satan and his practices, Jesus was able to identify those that are related to Satan.

Profilers work to predict future actions based on past behaviors. This tedious and time-consuming job can be daunting. If not handled properly, murderers, thieves, and the likes thereof will continue to roam our world, causing havoc to our lives. We see the importance of the information extrapolated from an individual's past and how damaging it can be if not analyzed properly.

After beginning with such an offensive statement, Jesus continues to tell those gathered around Him that *...and the lust of your father will ye do.* Here, Jesus charges the crowd with working for the devil. Furthermore, He links them to the devil through paternity. Jesus was able to come to this conclusion using the information provided by these people themselves.

Consider the Source

Throughout the entire chapter up until this point, the people have argued against that which Jesus spoke, taught, and ministered.

As Jesus makes known their relationship to the devil, He then confronts the crimes of their father. Jesus states, *He was a murderer from the beginning, and abode not in the truth, because there is no truth in him.* The occurrence Jesus refers to is portrayed in Genesis 3.

In Genesis 3, we find the account of the temptation and ultimate fall of mankind. By utilizing deductive reasoning, we can agree that this event meets the criteria as a point of reference. The temptation of man happened in the beginning and was the first evidenced occurrence concerning mankind after his creation. In the text, we find the serpent lying to Eve in Genesis 3:4, *Ye shall not surely die.* Given that his statement is the first of many of the devil's lies recorded in scripture, Jesus is furthermore correct in deeming Satan as the "father of it". Furthermore, Jesus calls Satan a murderer. Satan's efforts and man's self-will consequently brought the consequence of death to the whole world for ages to come. (Romans 5:12) The term murderer would apply to the serpent, which according to Genesis 3, tempted Eve. The actions of the serpent in the Garden of Eden would therefore fit the description of the devil provided by Jesus in John 8:44. Moreover, we can find no other event in Biblical history that would fit the description of the devil than that found in Genesis 3. We also find a supporting truss between the serpent (Genesis 3) and the devil (John 8:44) in Revelations 12:9 and 20:2.

> *And the great dragon was cast out, that old serpent, called the Devil, and Satan, which deceiveth the whole world: he was cast out into the earth, and his angels were cast out with him.* ~ Rev. 12:9
>
> *And he laid hold on the dragon, that old serpent, which is the Devil, and Satan, and bound him a thousand years.* ~ Rev. 20:2

The name Satan means an adversary-primarily to God and secondarily to men. The name devil suggests that he is a slanderer of God to men, and of men to God. Now that the information has been extrapolated about the devil's past crimes, Jesus shifts to His closing arguments in his case against the devil and his children.

Satan is full of nothing but lies. Every word that he speaks is a lie because there is nothing in him but lies. Jesus lets us know that the devil does not live or have residence in truth. As you recall, Satan was kicked out of Heaven. In Isaiah 14, we find that his expelling was due to his own inability to accept that God is the Most High and must be respected as such. As a believer in Christ fighting the good fight of faith, we ought to understand Satan's Modi Operandi. The Modi Operandi is the modes of operation used by the devil in an attempt to separate the believer from God's divine purpose for their life. Jesus, in John 8:44 and John 10:10, identifies the modes of operation utilized by the enemy. Jesus, in our central text for this literary work, first acknowledges that Satan is a murderer; secondly, He makes known his lifestyle of living outside of truth, and then He identifies his tendency to lie.

In John 10:10, we find that Jesus further explains the modes of operation of Satan. *The thief cometh not, but for to steal, and to kill, and to destroy: I am come that they might have life, and that they might have it more abundantly.* Satan's modes of operation are to steal from the believer, to kill the believer, and to destroy the believer. In its simplest form, Satan does not want to see us succeed in a relationship with Jesus Christ. Given all that we now know about the enemy we have to purpose in our hearts to break free from his lies. Thus we must consider our enemy, grab hold to our spiritual weapons of warfare, and proceed into battle. By understanding what and who we fight against, it can, at times, make our battle a little easier.

In the next few chapters I will share with you four lies that the devil has presented to me, and my personal testimony of overcoming his lies. I will then share instructions that God has given to remain free from the subjugation of Satan's lies.

Chapter 3

A STRUGGLE OVER LOVE

Life has an eerie way of bringing out what's in our hearts and minds. In my times of struggle and despair, Satan presented me with this lie. God doesn't love you. The test of overcoming this lie was a huge struggle for me because of all that I had been through. Satan knew just what button to push to take me over the edge and oftentimes, I didn't recognize I'd been under attack until it was all over.

Growing up, I often heard the musical classic by Tina Turner playing, "What's Love Got to Do with It?" Preachers, with their Bibles in tote, would always respond on Sunday morning: "Everything!" Being born

A Struggle Over Love

to a mother who was stricken with a mental impairment and an absent father presented a plethora of challenges. Life, from a natural eye, has not been the greatest for me; but from a spiritual eye, neither was it the worst.

As a result of my mother's condition for most of my life, I lived with my grandmother, who cared for and provided my parental needs and guidance. I grew up in a three-family structure home in urban Detroit. My grandmother did all she could to provide for me. I can recall many times when finances would run low and my grandmother would roll coins to send me to the grocery store with to purchase household necessities. Nevertheless, we somehow made it through those hard times. Knowing the struggle of the house only added to my feelings of self pity.

The challenges of life caused me to sometimes feel that God didn't love me. I felt alone, abandoned, angry and ashamed. I can recall one day when I was in the first grade; students in my class were asked to bring their parents to class with them. At

A Struggle Over Love

first, I was ashamed to have my mom come, because most of the kids knew of her impairment and I feared they would make fun of me or her. Though, with the help of my grandmother and an aunt, she showed up and it was one of the best moments in my life. I was finally seeing some sunlight in my life. However, despite that small ray of sunlight; it didn't change the feelings of neglect and abandonment that I felt, nor did it take away the shame.

Challenges as a teenager brought thoughts of suicide and running away from home. The feelings of not being loved continued to manifest. As I grew older, when things went haywire in my life, immediately without thought, I said within my heart, *God doesn't love me.*

I've found that life has an eerie way of bringing out what's in our hearts and minds. In my times of struggle and despair, Satan presented me with this lie. *God doesn't love you.* The test of overcoming this lie was a huge struggle for me because of all that I had been through. Satan knew just what button to push to take me over the edge and oftentimes, I didn't recognize I'd been under attack until it was all over. My mind had become bombarded with thoughts of evil, suicide, and leaving Christ. I became isolated within, walking around like a living dead, because in my mind, there was no use for me in this world.

I was fully entangled in the lies of the enemy. It wasn't until that day I was sitting in the hospital room, blood sugar extremely elevated, feeling frustrated, angry, and tired that I heard the Holy Spirit speak to me and say, *For God so loved YOU that he gave His only begotten Son*. In that moment, I doubted if in fact God was speaking to me, but soon confirmation and revelation came.

The Holy Spirit within me confirmed that I was hearing the voice of God and provided revelation as to what I was hearing in that moment. The revelation was that what I was feeling, saying, and hearing about *God not* loving me was a lie from the enemy.

A Struggle Over Love

The devil's attack against me was designed to deceive me into believing that God did not love me. He capitalized on the fact that there were countless times in my life where I felt everyone around had left me alone. Satan was aware of those times when I didn't feel loved by my family, friends, or God. In those times I would pray to God, but before the prayer was over, I doubted if He had even heard me.

Reflecting now, one passage of scripture that come to mind is in Job, chapter 23. This Old Testament man of God went through some hard times. Through his trials he dealt with what so many of us deal with today. We feel hurt, left out, depressed, demoralized, and shameful. It is in those times that Satan presents his lie that God does not love us. In Job 23: 8-9, we find Job searching for, what seems to be, a distant Savior. I too found myself searching, however unlike Job all through my search, I seemed to be losing faith in God's love.

As I look around today, the headlines all read just about the same: foreclosures, job cuts, layoffs, and stocks down. It seems like there is no hope. In Job 23:10; I see Job having some audacious hope that soon God would come and work out his situation. The Bible records that while in his time of testing Job's wife encouraged him to curse God and die. Job, in turn, called her a fool. During Job's testing he was mocked by men, but yet he kept the faith. He lost his home, family, riches, and even his status in the world, but he remained hopeful and faithful to God. Because of his hope and faithfulness in and to God, he was rewarded with double for his trouble. Even in the end result we see God's love at work.

Through my prayers and time of study I have learned that God's love is so powerful and widespread. The Bible says in Ephesians 2:4, *But God, who is rich in mercy, for his great love wherewith he loved us...!* God, who is rich in mercy, forgiveness, and compassion decided to love us with His great love. Because of this truth, I have since learned to tell the devil he is a liar. God does love me, and to prove His love for me, He sent His only begotten Son to die on the cross for my sins and to

A Struggle Over Love

give me double for my trouble. Despite the fact that I would still rebel and sin, disobey and neglect, he yet sent His Son to die for me. He died a gruesome death, one not fitting for an animal, but He did it all for my sake.

Jesus died to show forth the love of God to a loveless world. Now that I know the truth in my times of despair, I do as the Word says and run to the name of the Lord. *The name of the LORD is a strong tower: the righteous runneth into it, and is safe.* (Proverbs 18:10) As a believer, I now know that I don't have to struggle with whether God loves me nor do I have to struggle with the enemy. I have Christ as my perfect picture of love that can dispel any lie from the devil concerning God's love for me. The agape love of God is such a great thing.

Through God's love, we can become free and victorious over the lies and schemes of the enemy and his imps. The Bible on a number of occasions gives us undeniable evidence of the devil's tactics and plan to make us feel that God does not love us. There in the Garden of Eden. The serpent tells Eve to eat

A Struggle Over Love

from the tree saying, *thou shall not surely die.* However, we know that God commanded Adam and Eve not to eat from the tree because they would die. The devil in the Garden wanted Eve to believe that God was lying to her, therefore showing a lack of love for her.

In our lives today, the devil is using the same tactics. The devil tells us *its ok to sin everyone's doing it.* He urges us on saying, *You will not surely die.* Nonetheless, if we yield to the enemy's tactics, we put ourselves in a position of vulnerability. Consequently we begin to question God's love for us and the struggle over love ensues. After discovering truth I made up my mind to tell the devil he's a liar, and my struggle over love ends with my declaration of this fact: For God so loved the world [ME], He gave His only begotten Son.

Chapter 4

A Place Called Rehoboth

I hear God saying, "No matter how tough the attacks get, don't give up your possessions." The lies of the devil will make us feel as if we have to give up our possessions to make it through our feelings of loneliness.

So now, I've become free from this struggle over love, only to feel like I have nowhere to turn. Being the child of a mother with a mental impairment would have been enough but add to the mixture an absent father and the batter thickens. Have you ever felt like a nomad--just traveling across the sands of time, just passing day by day, here today and gone tomorrow? Perhaps you've even felt like there was no place made for you.

I tried to attend college to acquire a degree within the four years, but that didn't work. I interviewed for a job, was offered the position, started the first day, but then I felt out of place. I've been told that in life, we all go through a period of wandering. I believe that. What, where, when, how, and sometimes why are the questions we ask. What will God have me to do in this life? Where will God have me to do this? When will God have me to do this? How will God have me to do this? And yes, sometimes the question even becomes *why* will God have me to do this? The devil's lies are all poised to make us feel helpless and alone. The devil would have us to believe that in our times of distress, we have no one to turn to. Moreover, his lies will make us feel as if our wheels are just spinning.

We spend a countless amount of precious time wandering and looking for a place to belong, fit in, or just thrive.

I recall how after hearing my call to ministry I spent so much time trying to understand exactly what this meant. Intellectually, I understood and comprehended that there was a calling, but I didn't understand exactly what it was and what precisely I would be doing. Even today as I pen these words, I have yet to fully comprehend what God would have me to do in its fullest definition. Nevertheless, you and I have to proceed in faith knowing that he is faithful that promised.

A few years ago I shared the news of my call to the ministry with a spiritual leader; I told him that I felt the call to the ministry upon my life. I shared how I wrestled with verbalizing this feeling because of fear. I feared being rejected; being told that I was wrong or that I hadn't heard God.

Weeks before I shared this conversation, I asked the Lord some questions regarding my call to the ministry. I asked God those when, where, how and why questions. My motivation to question God was fear. Reflecting now, my former feelings of abandonment wouldn't allow my faith to receive that God actually had a place for me in his kingdom work. Seeking God in prayer the Spirit of the Lord led me to Genesis 26; there I would find the answers that I sought.

In this particular passage of scripture we find the story of Isaac. Isaac was the promised son of Abraham and Sarah. Isaac is the second of whom the Covenant of God is kept with, the first being his father Abraham, and the third being Isaac's son Jacob. Thus we have the well-known line in every church: "God made a promise with Abraham, Isaac and Jacob." According to the text, a famine strikes the land and Isaac, in search of supply, purposes in his heart to go to Egypt. However, the Lord appeared unto him and told him not to go to Egypt, but instead to go to the land of Gerar and dwell there. Isaac had initially settled near Beerlahairoi, where his sons Esau and Jacob were born. The famine, however, drove him to Gerar. Gerar was a land occupied by the Philistines. The Philistines would become Israel's fiercest enemy. Although they appeared friendly to Isaac, we find in other passages of the Bible that these people battled with Israel in the time of Joshua, The Judges, and David. In obedience to God, Isaac, along with his wife, goes to Gerar and they dwell in the land. In fear for his safety and for that of his wife, Isaac tells the townspeople that Rebekah, his wife, is his sister. Isaac told this to King Abimelech and the men of the town who inquired about her. However, there came a day when the king observed from his window Isaac and Rebekah *sporting* with each other or, as one version puts it, "making love."

After observing this, the king confronts Isaac. Isaac confesses about his fear and King Abimelech, out of anger, scolds Isaac for his actions. The text goes on to say that Isaac sowed in that land and received in the same year a hundredfold and he was blessed of the Lord. Then again, King Abimelech came to Isaac, and requested him to leave his land because he had become so blessed that the people saw him as being inferior to them. Isaac packed his things and went and dwelt in the Valley of Gerar. Due to the location of the land that he dwelt in, water was of great necessity and the Philistines knew it. Out of spite, the jealous Philistines plugged the wells that had been previously dug by Abraham, Isaac's father. Moreover, they strove with Isaac and his servants over several of the wells that they had dug out. Each time Isaac and his men would dig a well, the Philistines fought with Isaac over the well. In Genesis 26:22, the Bible records that Isaac and his servants dug a well and strove not over it and Isaac named the well "Rehoboth," meaning, "the well of room enough for us at last."

In our lives we will all have to strive over some things. There were many days when I felt like Isaac, and even now in this season of my life, I sometimes feel like him. God has commanded me to do something, go somewhere, but every time I make a move, it seems like something's blocking me. Isaac followed God's directions; nevertheless, there were hiccups along the way. I have discovered in my short walk with Christ that the devil will place people, things, affections, and emotions in our path to distract us and attempt to steal our blessings.

Isaac was not a poor or needy man. The Bible tells us how he sowed in the land and reaped significantly. He could have easily traded some of his possessions for one of the wells. I hear God saying, "No matter how tough the attacks get, don't give up your possessions." The lies of the devil will make us feel as if we have to give up our possessions to make it through our feelings of loneliness. We give up our friends, our family, our jobs, our education, and our right to eternal life all because of a lie. In our times of loneliness and struggle, that old sneaky serpent swarms himself into our thoughts and says, *God doesn't have a place for you.*

Being so entangled in Satan's lie, I have gone as far as to change jobs, cars, the styles of clothes I wear, and even how I cut my hair. However, nothing I did in the natural stopped his lie. I imagine that Isaac after awhile got agitated with the fights over the wells. He was probably saying to himself, *I dug this well and spent my time grooming it, and then someone comes and takes it.*

Although, it wasn't a natural well that I was fighting over, I've felt these emotions before. I recall one night praying to God about how upset I was about my life, and how I was tired of everyone and everything and how I wanted to end it all. The devil was right there with his lie, *God doesn't have a place for you.* He was there adding fuel to the fire. Spewing every vicious lie he could at me, because Satan knew better than I did, that if I waited on God long enough he'd make room for me.

Today I rejoice in letting you know that contrary to what the devil says God has a place for us and he will provide it. Philippians 4:19 says, *But my God shall supply all of your need according to his riches in glory by Christ Jesus.* The Bible says, *Eye hath not seen, nor ear heard, neither have entered into the heart of man, the things which God hath prepared for them that love him.* (1 Corinthians 2:9) Just like He did for Isaac, God has made a promise to bless me, to prosper me, and to provide for me. He is Jehovah Jireh, the Lord our provider. In a moment of prayer, I told the devil that he is a liar. God *has* prepared a place

A Place Called Rehoboth

for me. He has prepared a place called "Rehoboth", meaning the well of room enough for us at last. Just when it seemed like the fight was over, King Jesus stepped in the ring and with one swing, has knocked the competition out cold. God, through Jesus Christ, came to be that well of room enough for us at last. Our sinful nature had separated us from the love of God. Our spiritual telephones had been disconnected and we could not communicate with Heaven any longer.

In an attempt to draw closer to God and receive atonement for our sins, humanity sacrificed animals and other burnt offerings before the Lord. However, true atonement could only be made through the shedding of pure blood. God sent his Son to come and make room for us. Our telephone lines were reconnected and our service was restored. Not only has God, through Jesus Christ, restored our service, but He has sent a comforter, the Holy Spirit, to serve as an on-board maintenance worker. Finally, Jesus told us that He has gone to prepare a place for us, that where He is we may be also.

A Place Called Rehoboth

God does have a place for us. Jeremiah 29:11 says, *For I know the thoughts that I think toward you, saith the Lord, thoughts of peace, and not of evil, to give you an expected end.* I have since cursed those feelings of isolation, fear, anger; defeat and unbelief back to the pit of hell and told the devil he is a liar. By this truth we must overcome the struggle over love to be received to this place called "Rehoboth" and our declaration that the devil is a liar has freed us to enjoy it. Embrace *this new* place!

Chapter 5

HELP! I'VE FALLEN. CAN I GET UP?

Finally, I was away from the pool. It was in that most challenging time that I began to hear the Lord say, Rise, take up thy bed, and walk.

Life is not always fair. Sometimes we are dealt a jacked up hand of cards to play with. Perhaps you've been forced to play with a deck that is missing a few cards; nevertheless, the game is in full swing. Play your hand! We've heard it said time and again that you can't hold a good man or woman down; they will soon rise above it all. Through falsehoods, old wise tales, and even misinterpretation, some of us have believed the contrary. I believe this is so because the devil works so hard to convince us that we can't get up or be freed from our present state or situation.

John 5 details the story of a man who lay at the Pool of Bethesda. This man is said to have had an infirmity for thirty-eight years. Can you imagine the repercussions of having an ailment for thirty-eight years? Sitting in the same spot for thirty-eight years! I would imagine that this man's life was wrecked by his debilitating issue. Here is a man that is forced to spend his days, and possibly even nights, lying next to a pool, waiting on an angel to come and deliver his divine opportunity for deliverance. The implications of his circumstances are monumental. I'm sure he felt demoralized, ashamed, and possibly even suicidal.

The Bible records that Jesus came into Jerusalem for the Feast of the Jews. This is one of three feasts that required all males to come to Jerusalem. All of the brothers of the community came home, most of them in a celebratory fashion. Along with them are their families, and they are meeting their friends in the street. As they approach this pool, I imagine that the man knew some of them and they stopped for a second to chat about their lives, only to walk away perplexed as to why he remained in the same place as where they had last saw him. This had to be a hard place for him to be. The location of his fall wasn't helping his status either.

The Bible speaks of this pool that sat near the sheep market that was called, in the Hebrew tongue, Bethesda because it had five porches. It is worth noting that in Biblical numerology, the number five is said to be the number of grace. Grace means favor! There are many kinds of favor. Favor that is shown to the miserable can be called mercy, while favor shown to the poor is often called pity. However, favor shown to the unworthy is called grace. This is favor indeed, favor that is certainly divine in its source and its character.

Help! I've Fallen. Can I Get Up?

It was said of the Pool of Bethesda that an angel would come at a certain season and trouble the water; whoever got in the water first after the troubling was made whole of their disease. This man, and others with infirmities similar to his, found themselves sitting by this pool, waiting on an angel. So now comes Jesus into the town and He observes these people lying around waiting. The Bible says that they were impotent, blind, halt, and withered. They were all waiting on an angel. Jesus takes note of this man. I like to believe that Jesus, before even speaking to the man was aware of how long he had been in that condition. Jesus looks at the man and in John 5:6, asks him a question; *Wilt thou be made whole?* I imagine that the man ignored Jesus, perhaps supposing that He was just another passerby who was looking to make fun of him. Perhaps he had become disgruntled by the presence of all of the men in the community and their stares and smart remarks. Maybe he felt helpless when asked the question.

Help! I've Fallen. Can I Get Up?

His response to Jesus further lets me know that he did feel helpless and hopeless that he could ever get a change in his situation. The scripture says that the man tells Jesus that when the water is troubled, he has no one to put him in, and when he tries on his own, someone steps in front of him. Jesus, appearing not to care about his excuses says; *Rise, take up thy bed, and walk.* (John 5:8) The Bible says that immediately the man got up and took that which he laid on and carried it. How awesome it is to be able to get up from where we have fallen and wasted so much time! Deeper than that, you might think that this man would have some trouble walking after being in the same shape for thirty-eight years. I submit to you that Jesus' words not only healed his physical ailment, but also his mental ailment. Immediately, he got up and carried his bed.

Not too long ago in my own life, I was just like this man lying at the pool, waiting on an angel. A young newlywed and life was good, but a few months into my marriage, my wife and I began caring for my mom and brother. The four of us lived together in one home for three years. Throughout the years, things started to go wrong with the house, my health, my life, and my relationship with Christ. But I kept lying there, waiting for an angel.

It was a warm, rainy day in July when I got home from church to find that the sewage system had backed up into the house and the smell was awful. I called the leasing company and they pretty much said that I was on my own. I found a plumber, got the repairs done, and resumed lying by the pool. The next year, I came home from work to find a large hole in the ceiling due to roof damage. Water was everywhere, but again, I kept lying there. I contacted the leasing company and they made promises that never were served.

A few weeks later, my wife called me at work in a panic because my brother was being out of control in a psychotic rage, hollering out threatening statements. I left work, admitted him to the local psychiatric facility, and went back to lie down next to the pool. Another year passed filled with the same types of incidents; but through it all, I kept waiting on an angel or so I thought.

It's worth noting that during this waiting season, I was attending church faithfully, tithing consistently, and giving offering and serving as a leader in the church. Furthermore, I, just like this man, was observing my fellow brothers returning from their lives in a celebratory fashion, all while I continued to lie down next to the pool. The second year of my waiting for an angel, I was laid off from work, was searching for a job, and all at the same time, was in failing health. I struggled to make ends meet for an entire year. Verbally saying I was trusting God but in all actuality I wasn't.

Nearly a year later, I left home one Friday for a job interview and it went well. I stopped by the church to see my former pastor and talk with him. As we talked, he asked, "Son, are you ok?" I responded in my usual tone, "Of course," but I wasn't. Later that evening, I went into the emergency room and found that I had a blood sugar level of 586. The doctors rushed me to the back and there I remained for the entire weekend. Finally, I was away from the pool. It was in that most challenging time that I began to hear the Lord say, *When you've had enough*. My moment of challenge had become my moment of preparation for transition. The Lord began to instruct me to *Rise, take up thy bed, and walk.* For three years, I had been managing a family, work, school, and caring for ill relatives. The only reason I continued trying to do it was because of a lie that the enemy told me: *You can't get up from here.* My wife and I would talk about the changes we wanted to make, but there was always something within me saying, *You can't get up* I thank God for my wife and her ability to pray, because I'm sure she wanted to leave a brother many days but she honored her vows and prayed that soon, I'd get us out.

Thanks to God, I finally did get up. After spending the weekend in the hospital, I got a call that I had been chosen for the position I had interviewed for that past Friday. In the next few weeks, I was blessed to find a new home for my wife and me. In addition, my mother and brother were now being taken care of in their own place of residence. All this was done in approximately four weeks. I took God at His Word and placed everything in His hands.

So many times we wait for an angel to do what we have already been empowered to do. Jesus never touched the man, he simply spoke the Word to him. My brothers and sisters, the devil works diligently to infuse into our minds a spirit of defeat. Using lies about our home life, finances, health, and mental status, the enemy keeps us down, lying near the pool waiting on an angel. Consequently, we never think about the potential of seeing Jesus and receiving our miracle. My mind had become so focused on receiving my deliverance one way that I failed to realize the *Godtunities* presented to me.

Godtunites are those moments in life when your back is against the wall and you seemingly have nowhere to turn. Those moments of sickness, death, despair, poverty and destruction. In those moments, you've just entered a Godtunity. Some call them miracle moments, because the likelihood of a miracle is greater. I call them Godtunities because the likelihood of God giving you the power to change the situation is greater.

Romans 8:37 says, *Nay, in all things we are more than conquerors through him that loved us.* Just like this man who was lying by the pool, we can get up. Satan plots to keep us trapped below the surface of potential and possibility. He seeks to shield our eyes from the truth that with Jesus Christ, we can rise above our obstacles, circumstances, hurts, and problems. Jesus, in John 10:10 declared ...*I am come that they might have life, and that they might have it more abundantly.* Today cast the spirit of defeat back to the pit of hell where it came from. I plead the blood of Jesus over our lives. We are indeed the head and not the tail, above only and not beneath. No weapon that is formed against us shall be able to prosper, for greater is He that is in us than he that is in the world. Through our fight to overcome the struggle over love, and then entering a place called Rehoboth, God has laid the foundation for us to get up from where we lay. No more can we remain where we are. Awake, awake, awake O' Zion and put on your strength for the Lord is near.

Chapter 6

YOU DON'T QUALIFY

I remember sitting there listening as the pastor gave his all-too-familiar speech about hell, eternity, your soul, and Jesus. In an attempt to distract myself, I began fidgeting with my socks. Soon, I found my feet moving down the center aisle of the church, headed for the front.

The devil has been so strategic in his attempt to distract us from receiving the gift of salvation found only through Jesus Christ. This is the one area where Satan launches his most vigorous attack. Undoubtedly, we understand why he is so fierce in his attacks against the knowledge and acceptance of Jesus Christ. Regardless of all of the imps and demonic angels he has, Satan would love nothing better than to see the creative handy work of God descend into hell with him. I have come to learn that regardless of popular opinion, Satan is not after my job, home, money, health, friends, or any other thing that I can hold dear to my heart. Instead, the enemy is after my relationship with Christ Jesus. He uses the aforementioned things to distract us and cause us to fear and doubt God's power in our lives.

The Bible affirms in Revelations 12:9 and 20:2-3 how the devil and his angels suffered being outcast and imprisoned to a bottomless pit. It is my theological opinion that the devil would love no more than to have millions of others to join him in his bottomless pit called hell. As a result, the enemy is attacking the church and its ministry of reconciliation in large numbers and, in some cases, on a larger scale. We can turn on our televisions and see how the enemy is in an all-out-assault on the church. The values and virtues held up by the church are

You Don't Qualify

constantly under attack by politicians and pundits alike. Several of the hot topics revolve around the institution of marriage and abortion. These attacks, I believe, only seek to destroy the foundation of our belief and to discourage men and women from seeking a relationship with Christ Jesus. Moreover, Satan seeks to present the relationship with Jesus as an unattainable position. He works eagerly to make us feel like we don't deserve a relationship with Jesus Christ. Therefore, we become so much more focused on our sins and shortcomings that we fail to see God's grace is sufficient to us.

The lie that the enemy continued to repeat to me was, *You don't qualify.* I was told I didn't qualify to be saved, have the job I have, live in the city I live in, drive the car I drive and I was told I didn't qualify to write a book. These statements came off the lips of people that Satan was using to distract me from my purpose. Satan is always trying to make us feel like we don't qualify. He constantly reminds us of our sins in hopes of deterring us from going to God through Jesus for redemption.

You Don't Qualify

Sin is not some foreign thing to me. There have been times in my life that I have fallen short in my walk with Christ. Sin has had its field days with me and in some instances, field nights, too. While in this state of sin, Satan wanted me to believe that I didn't qualify for a relationship with Christ Jesus. Satan has worked to make men and women feel that they don't qualify for the blessing and miracle of salvation. I can remember the day I accepted Jesus as my Lord and Savior.

I remember sitting there listening as the pastor gave his all-too-familiar speech about hell, eternity, your soul, and Jesus. In an attempt to distract myself, I began fidgeting with my socks. Soon, I found my feet moving down the center aisle of the church, headed for the front. As I walked, Satan reminded me of all of my sins. *You are a liar, you curse, you listen to secular music, and you're a thief.* He was just rattling them off at me, but something caused me to keep walking. As I reminisce about my walk of faith, John 3:16 falls into my spirit. The Bible says, *For God so loved the world that he gave his only begotten Son, that whosoever believeth in him should not perish, but have everlasting life.* For a long time, I did not know how to fight against the enemy's lie about my qualification for salvation. However, as I studied God's Word, I found clearly that my qualification for the miracle of salvation had nothing to do with me at all. Truth is that before I came to Christ, I was guilty of all of the charges that Satan had placed upon me. I was guilty as charged. However, the blood covered me. Yes, the blood of Jesus covers our sins and when death should be our sentence, life now becomes the judgment.

Even after I gave my life to the Lord, I found myself falling short of His glory. I would lie, cheat, steal, curse and do other unimaginable things that displeased God. But, God who is rich in mercies forgave me. I repented to him and he forgave my trespasses. Because of this second chance I work daily to live a holy life before the Lord.

Yet, my qualification for salvation had nothing to do with me. It is because of God, in His awesomeness, He knew that I would need salvation and therefore, He sent his only Son to die on the cross for my sins. What qualifies us for salvation is simply God's love for us even while we were yet sinners. My response to the lie from the devil that tells me that I don't qualify is that the Word of God says otherwise.

I thank God for His breadth. He is a God that has no respect of persons and he is not restricted by time or any other thing. With God all things are possible. And his grace, wow let me tell you about his grace. God's grace is so sufficient because it is rooted in love that it can cover a multitude of sins. That means that the murderer, child rapist, thief, liar, backbiter, homosexual and yes, even the fallen politicians can be forgiven. Due to the blood of Jesus, all who confess Jesus as Lord can receive salvation. God, who is rich in mercy, promises to forgive our sins and trespasses and He washes us clean.

I'm encouraged daily cast that lie back to the pit of hell to its originator and declare in the name of Jesus that indeed, if any man or woman call upon the name of the Lord, they shall be saved. Through God's love and his Word, we have overcome the struggle over love, found a place of room enough at last for us, discovered we can arise from our fallen places, and now we find that we indeed do qualify. It's awesome to know the truth and it surely makes us free from the lies of Satan and his imps.

Chapter 7

THE STAGE OF CONCRETIZATION

Therefore, we discover a sincere need to fortify our victory over the lies of Satan. Through the Word of God, we have been given a formula on how to handle Satan.

The task at hand as we move forward is that we must fortify our victory. We have overcome the struggle with love, embraced our place in God, got up and received our statement of qualification, but that's half the battle. A military drill sergeant once shared with me that the second most significant job of a military unit is to fortify their victory.

The Stage of Concretization

This is concretization. Concretization is the process by which a thought or action becomes concrete.

What good is it for us to reclaim surrendered or captured soil, only to leave access for the enemy to return? The Bible declares that once an evil spirit has been removed, the keeper of the house will sweep the house clean. However, there will come a time when the strong spirit will say to itself that he will return to his house, and will do so with seven times the strength as before. Therefore, we discover a sincere need to fortify our victory over the lies of Satan.

Through the Word of God, we have been given a formula on how to handle Satan. Jesus, in Matthew, Chapter 4, provides us with a concrete formula. This chapter details Satan's tempting of Jesus in the wilderness during His forty days of fasting. Time after time, Satan poses to Jesus, what we might consider in the flesh, a worthwhile deal. Nevertheless, Jesus in His awesomeness responds to each proposition with the Word of God. Here we discover that the only true way to handle the liar

The Stage of Concretization

is to use the Word of God. David, in Psalm 119:11, says to the Lord, *Thy word have I hid in mine heart, that I might not sin against thee.* Satan's propositions come in the form of lies and the goal of each is only to cause us to sin against God. When we begin to apply the Word of God to situations, we are able to determine that it's all a lie. When we try the spirit, whether it be of God or not, we are able to see its true nature. The lies of Satan can never stand against the truth of God.

The Bible declares that we are to put on the whole armor of God that we can stand against the wiles or schemes of the devil. This is the second weapon in our arsenal against the lies of Satan. We are to gird our loins with truth. Then we are to wear the breastplate of righteousness. The breastplate is the one piece of battle wear that is easily seen by our enemy and usually has an insignia on it. The shield identifies who you are and whose you are. We are to put on the shoes of the gospel of peace. Therefore, no matter where we walk, we should bring to the situation a peace with us. We are then to carry with us the shield

The Stage of Concretization

of faith. This shield will provide protection for us when the enemy launches his many darts at us in an attempt to destroy us. We are then charged with putting on the helmet of salvation. This piece of armor protects our thinking, symbolizing the newness of our minds since being in Christ Jesus. Finally, we are to take with us the sword of the spirit, the Word of God. This sword is our weapon of mass destruction against the enemy. This weapon is powerful and sharper than any two-edged sword.

Just as Jesus exemplified in His wilderness experience, we must handle the liar with the Word of God. When the enemy puts doubt into our minds concerning the promises of God, we must begin to doubt the doubt. You read correctly. Doubt the doubt. When the enemy says you are not blessed, tell him that God said you are. When the enemy says you're sick, tell him that you're healed. Doubt the doubt. There are many lies that the enemy will use to confuse and distract us from receiving what God has for us. Whether the lie is concerning God's love for us, direction for our lives, help in our distress, or eligibility to

The Stage of Concretization

receive salvation, we must remain firm in our convictions and the teachings of Jesus as found in John 8:44. Nothing true can ever come from the enemy, thus when he speaks, we should at no time take to heart his words. They are rooted in deceit and murder and aim to separate us from God. As you continue in your period of concretization please consider the next chapter that discusses five pillars of victory that will lead to continuous victory over the lies of the devil. God's truth will make us free.

Chapter 8

FIVE PILLARS TO SECURE VICTORY

Prayer & Confession; Obeying the Voice of God; Trusting in the Lord; Walking by Faith; Grabbing Hold to your Cross

Pillar 1-Prayer & Confession

Although this seems to be two in one, they are actually vastly intertwined. Prayer coincides with confession because it is only in our private time with God that we are willing to share our innermost secrets, faults, and appreciations to God. It is at this time that we *...come boldly unto the throne of grace that we may obtain mercy, and find grace to help in time of need.* (Hebrews 4:16) In our private time of prayer, we are more apt to tell God about our troubles and the areas we need help in. In an effort to remain free from the devil's lies, it is imperative that we have a prayer life.

I have discovered that there were times when I failed to pray about a particular situation I was going through and before long it had developed to an overwhelming stature. I had aborted the only answer to my problem... prayer. Jesus taught the disciples in Matthew 6:9-13 how to pray. We need to sometimes go back and revisit this profound passage of scripture. Here we will discover God's principles of prayer.

David in the Psalms rendered many prayers unto God, some of praise, some for help, and others of gratefulness. Just as David, no matter where we find ourselves in this life, we must continually seek the Lord's face in prayer. Matthew 6:33 encourages us to seek ye first the Kingdom of God and his righteousness and all these things shall be added unto us. While prayer is a prerequisite, in order to be sure that our prayers are heard, we must practice confession.

David, in Psalm 51:10, asks the Lord, *Create in me a clean heart. O God; and renew a right spirit within me.* Theology has discovered and determined that this particular Psalm was written during the period of David's affair with Bathsheba. Confession is a necessity. Even in what we know as The Lord's Prayer, a significant verse is Matthew 6:12: *And forgive us our debts, as we forgive our debtors.* This verse implies that constantly we must seek the Lord's forgiveness of our sins, and remember to forgive others.

Prayer and confession are essential elements to being free from the devil's lies. Prayer can seem to challenge our faith yet, it really should not. Luke 18:1 states, *men ought always to pray.*

Prayer is our communication with God and His Word is His communication with us. As in our personal, social, or collective relationships, the determining factor of how the relationship is progressing can be found in the value of its communication. Likewise, the factor that determines our

Five Pillars to Secure Victory

progression in a relationship with God is the value of our communication.

Personally it seemed very hard to pray at times. I would try to set aside time each day to pray; nonetheless, things would cause me to deter from my prayer time. Finally after taking a stand within myself and demanding that I pray (communicate with God), those things began to disappear. Our prayer (communication) time should always be priority to all other tasks, and within our communication, we must remember to practice confession. Maybe you say that you have nothing to confess, yet confession is not only done with regard to sin, but it is also done about our joys, confessing that you love God, confessing that you appreciate God. Some synonyms of the word confess are: to admit, to acknowledge, to declare, and to own up to. When I confess that I love God, I admit to it, I acknowledge it, I declare it, I own up to it. Confession is good for the soul of man and pleasant to the sight of God. *If we confess our sins, he is faithful and just to forgive us our sins, and to cleanse us from all unrighteousness.* (1 John 1:9)

Pillar 2-Obeying the Voice of God

The bible tells us that obedience is greater than sacrifice. The greatest blessing in obedience, I believe, is being able to remain whole. Throughout our lives, whenever we are obedient to God, everything seems to work in our favor. The children get up in the morning on time, the car runs better, and the bank account is always at a positive balance. Everything simply flows. God commanded Abraham to take his son Isaac and offer him up to the Lord. Abraham's devotion and obedience to the voice of God caused him to do as he was told. Abraham was prepared to sacrifice his only son, but God had a ram in the bush and Abraham's obedience was rewarded. Can you recall times when things in your life have happened because of your obedience… as well as disobedience? I can.

Recollecting about my care giving responsibilities, it was a little under three years, when the Lord instructed my wife and I to make a change. Honestly, when I initially heard the Word, fear and panic erupted in my mind. Reflecting now I call to remembrance the scripture 2 Timothy 1:7, *For God hath not given us the spirit of fear; but of power, and of love, and of a sound mind.*

Nonetheless, it took some time before I came to my senses and actually moved. When we moved, I began to feel a peace like never before. Those days of not sleeping turned into days full of rest. My wife and I finally were able to enjoy the company of each other without being interrupted by someone asking questions or going off into a psychotic rage. We finally were able to enjoy life.

It begs to ask, why was I so afraid of this? Satan had captured my thoughts and made me afraid to succeed. Even while writing this book, the enemy tried to discourage me: "You can't write a book. What can you share with others about God?" Nevertheless, I continued to write out of obedience because I recognize that God has a purpose and a plan for my writing.

Five Pillars to Secure Victory

If we are to remain free from the devil's lies, it is vital that we obey the voice and Word of God. The bible says, *The steps of a good man are ordered by the Lord.* (Psalm 37:23) In order for God to order our steps, we must be attentive to His voice. He that has an ear to hear, let him hear. What's more, not only must we be hearers, but also doers of the Word. What good is it for us to attend church every Sunday, hear the preached Word, pay our tithes, and sing a song, yet when we return home, we practice none of what was preached? The Bible talks about impudent and hardhearted people. (Ezekiel 3:7) Even when God sends a messenger to deliver a Word, they still refuse to obey and are just blatantly disrespectful to the voice and commands of God. Our obedience to the voice of God causes us to remain free from the devil's lies.

Remaining free is an essential reason why I obey the voice of the Lord, recognizing that whenever God commands me to do something, it is in an effort to make me whole or preserve my wholeness.

Five Pillars to Secure Victory

In Genesis 19, we read about Lot and his family who were commanded by the angels of the Lord to flee Sodom and Gomorrah because the Lord had sent them to destroy it. The angels told them to leave and not to look back, the Bible records that Lot's wife looked back. In verse 17, the angels commanded that they flee and not look back, or else they would be consumed. When God commands us to do a thing, it is only for our good and His glory. In seeking to remain free from the devil's lies, we must practice obeying the voice of God and regarding His Word as the final authority in all that we do.

Pillar 3-Trusting in the Lord

Trust in the Lord with all thine heart, and lean not unto thine own understanding, in all thy ways acknowledge him (God)*, and he* (God) *shall direct thy paths.* We have all heard it, we have even quoted it a few times, but do we practice it? Trust is something that I personally find hard to do. Don't get me wrong, I will trust when I can see everything that's happening, but asking me to trust blindly is truly a test for me.

In remaining free from the devil's lies, I found myself "smacked" in the face by the lack of trust I have put in God. I could easily give some excuses, but there are not any; I either trust or not. I thank God for how He continuously teaches me how important it is to trust Him. As I stated in the earlier section on obedience, when God spoke to me and said to make some changes, the number one reason I did nothing was because I did not trust God farther than I could see Him. I was too worried about provisions, perception, and longevity. Lord I want to move, but I don't have the money! Lord I want to move, but what will people think? Lord I want to move, but will it last forever or come crashing down on me?

My thoughts had been overtaken by fear--the number one attack of the enemy. My mouth was saying, "Lord I trust you," but my actions were saying, "I don't trust you." Granted, God had never let me down before, so why would He start now?

Five Pillars to Secure Victory

Trusting in the Lord cannot be a riddle that you recite or even a dance that you do, but it has to be an action that you take.

The fear of what might happen kept me constrained and locked up in my own personal prison with myself as the warden. I held the key to my own freedom; even so, I remained trapped by fear. It was when the Lord reiterated His Word to me that I finally woke up from my sleep of fear.

During a phone call with a dear friend, the Lord began to speak through him. As I was explaining the conditions of the house to him and how I hadn't worked in almost a year, he bluntly said, "Antoine, God is not pleased with you staying there in those conditions. Don't you know that God intends for us to be blessed, and not stressed? C'mon man, you know the Word. Activate your faith and trust in the Lord."

The house was unfit for anyone to occupy, not even the worst of animals. The roof leaked, there were plumbing problems, and the furnace did not operate properly. As I informed my friend about the issues, he responded with those words. I froze, and then a feeling of repentance overshadowed me. I had totally missed what God was saying all along.

Weeks before this phone call, the Lord asked if I trusted Him. I remained in the house because I thought I would have to find a job first, save some money, buy a car, and then move. God was not pleased with my living conditions and thought that I deserved better. After hearing those words from my friend, I prayed about it, talked with my wife, and then called the leasing company and told them that within the next thirty days, I would be moving. Without a job, money, new car, or even a prospective place to move, I just told the landlord of the house that I would be moving in thirty days. Talk about moving in faith!

It is my belief that my acts of faith spoke volumes to God. Within a short span of time God manifested so many blessings within a matter of weeks. My wife was blessed with a new job; I was blessed with a new job. My mother and brother were able to move into their own residence and be taken care of.

My wife and I found a nice place to move. As if he hadn't done enough, He made the move-in costs totally free to us! An individual who we knew blessed (not a loan, simply gave it to us) us with the finances to move in, and the first month's rent was free because of a special the leasing company was promoting. Favor isn't fair!

The actions taken by both my wife and I said to God, "We trust you." As a result, He blessed us exceeding, abundantly, above all that we could ask or think. That moment not only caused me to celebrate God's love for me, but it caused me to increase my trust in God. I challenge you that when those feelings of worry, fear, and distrust come believe God. Trusting in the Lord was a challenge for me; but as I grow in my faith trusting God is like breathing--it really doesn't take a lot of work, just do it.

Pillar 4-Walking By Faith

Some might contest that faith and trust in God are the same. I believe them to be two separate, yet equal, partners. In developing a relationship with God and remaining free from the lies of the enemy, I have come to find that a major ingredient in our walk with Christ is faith. *Now faith is the substance of things hoped for, the evidence of things not seen.* (Hebrews 11:1) Walking by faith has to be an anthem for one seeking to overcome the devil's lies. As with so many of the men and women of the Bible, God will give us a task to complete that requires activating our faith.

David, in 1 Samuel 17, went out up against a giant Philistine named Goliath. Although the facts stated that David would lose; although the thought in everyone's mind was to prepare for a funeral, David went out by faith and slew the Philistine. When we operate in faith, people will laugh at us and scorn us, even call us stupid; nonetheless, we have to remain steadfast in our faith. When I shared my vision of writing a book few people believed it could happen. The Lord spoke to me and said *hold on until you see what you saw.*

Five Pillars to Secure Victory

In remaining free from the devil's lies, I am learning to walk by faith and not by sight. I cannot be moved by the things that I see because sometimes our eyes play tricks on us. The Bible declares in Romans 8:24, *for we are saved by hope: but hope that is seen is not hope: for what a man seeth, why doth he yet hope for?* Faith and hope are siblings. You cannot have one without the other. If our hope is seen, then it is not hope.

Pillar 5-Grabbing A Hold to Your Cross

Jesus said, *Whosoever will come after me, let him deny himself, and take up his cross, and follow me.* (Mark 8:34-35) The cross that Jesus was referring to was not made of two by fours or tree trunks; instead, He is speaking of a spiritual cross. The cross represents the suffering, shame, trials, and tests that every believer will encounter, especially those seeking to remain free from the lies of the devil. So many times, I found myself asking God why I was going through a certain situation or when that trying situation would end. He seems to always answer back with the remark ...they *that wait upon the Lord*... (Isaiah 40:31)

In aligning ourselves to remain free, we must be prepared to be ridiculed, cast out, and cast down. More than that, we must be prepared to take up our cross. The Bible declares in Romans 8:18, *For I reckon that the sufferings of this present time are not worthy to be compared with the glory which shall be revealed in us.* So many times, we want to receive the blessings of following Christ, yet we despise the suffering associated with Him.

The Bible declares in Philippians 3:10, That *I may know him, and the power of his resurrection, and the fellowship of his sufferings, being made conformable unto his death.* It is worthy to point out that Paul, the writer, is saying that in knowing God, we must come to terms with His resurrection and suffering.

At the age of eighteen years old I thought I was on top of the world. Beautiful wife, home, job, attending school, just blessed. I was ready to take on the world and all it had to offer. I was living for Christ and making strides to get closer to him. I was exceedingly happy but this joyous time soon turned a little sorrowful, and would remain this way for a great deal of time. We had a new cross to bear. The ups and downs at times seemed too much to bear and so many days, we felt like giving up and throwing in the towel.

Being raised in the church, we understood the Word of God and we particularly appreciated the scripture in Romans 8:28, *And we know that all things work together for good to them that love God, to them who are the called according to his purpose.* In those trying three years, my wife and I suffered a lot. Yet, somehow we managed to keep our faith in God. I continue to point out this particular life experience because looking back some years later, we both recognized the test was our cross to bear at that time. When we further consider the events of our early years of marriage, we identify that it was during this point that we sought God for our purpose and destiny in life. Therefore we understand that God was getting the glory out of us back then and preparing us for a life of blessings. We now conclude that in seeking to remain free of the devil's lies, we must all be prepared to bear our cross.

In bearing our cross, we developed a little acronym that keeps us encouraged when times seem a little hard. For us the "CROSS" symbolizes: Christ Restoring Our Special Status. Christ had to endure much pain and hardship to restore our special status in this world. The initial plan of God was for man to live a life that was worthy of an heir to a king, free from all sin, and a life that was prosperous. In bearing the cross, Jesus restored our special status. Thus, in your bearing of the cross, Christ is restoring your special status. Just as gold has to go into the fire to become a flawless piece, we as Christians have to enter the fire to be refined and presented flawless. *But he knoweth the way that I take: when he hath tried me, I shall come forth as gold.* (Job 23:10) In life, we will face difficulties and come up against some hard troubles. Yet, we must remain encouraged that God has a perfect plan in play.

Chapter 9

A Final Word on Enough

Prayer & Confession; Obeying the Voice of God; Trusting in the Lord; Walking by Faith; Grabbing Hold to your Cross

Catastrophes, world conflicts, murders, thievery, embezzlement, and a host of unimaginable and senseless acts of negativity. There is so much happening in our world. With so much going on, it makes it easy for us to find ourselves bombarded and undergoing the battle of the mind. After life has dished us numerous blows and scars, we are left with clouded, cluttered, barraged minds that are no good.

A Final Word

Thus, we usher in high blood pressure, diabetes, stroke and innumerable other health issues. If we were honest with ourselves and each other, we would recognize that so many of us have been battling in our minds more than we have in our finances, relationships, schoolwork, housework, and relationship with Christ. Yet we make endless attempts at combating the aforementioned issues, but we never battle the root of the issue... the condition of our mind!

With all of this happening all around us, unless we connect with Christ, we undoubtedly will find ourselves overtaken by the wickedness of this world. It is my prayer to encourage your whole man (body, mind, soul and spirit) to seek a renewed mind through Christ and to challenge you to tell the devil he's a liar. As a Christian minister, it is my responsibility to share with my fellow brothers and sisters the revelation God has given me that has led to my conversion and propels me toward our loving Savior. I daily observe a world that is in crisis and the inhabitants are looking for answers. God is calling for us

A Final Word

to share with the world the good news of the Gospel and to tell the devil he's a liar. My prayer is to be led by the Spirit of God. Anything less is unacceptable.

So many of us find ourselves in a continuous battle with the enemy. We are feeling the constant blows of the enemy. Satan is filling the airwaves with lies and we face attacks on every side. But I can sense the Spirit of the Lord moving about and His anointing is falling, destroying these vicious lies that have become yolks of bondage upon the lives of so many of us. I encourage you to *stand fast in the faith, quit you like men, be strong.* (1 Corinthians 16:3) I encourage you who are in the Lord and even those who may have left the Lord, or are considering a return home. I share with you today that God loves you and He desires to have you with Him to fulfill His plan on the earth.

I speak to my brothers in the faith: Man, God needs you! I thank God for our women who have stood in the gap for so long. They've served as dual parents, protectors and providers, comforters and disciplinarians, but now it's high time that we

A Final Word

men confront the enemy. We must retake our position in our homes and in our communities. Our children our dying young, becoming parents young, and they are committing crimes young. We've got to do something quick.

I am aware that life, for many of us, has not been all sunshine and blue skies. There have been days, weeks, months, and maybe even years when we've felt abandoned by God. Times when we sat alone, wondering how the bills would be paid and how we would continue our education or protect our family. I believe that It was in those times that the enemy tiptoed into our thoughts and dreams and began to deposit his lies of deceit.

As you've read in the pages of this book, not too long ago, I found myself in this very place. But God! I heard the Lord speak to me, "When you've had enough, tell the devil he's a liar!"

As I studied the Word and sought God's revelation, I found peace in knowing that God's Word provided me with

A Final Word

ammunition and support to carry out the plan and win the battle. In my time of study, the Holy Spirit led me to the Gospel of John. There I found the answers and encouragement my soul desperately sought.

The Lord, through the Word, is daily teaching me to confront the enemy with the facts. The facts of God are sure and definite. God loves us despite what opposing opinions may say. God is qualifying, equipping, validating, and restoring strong men and women back to life for such a time as this. I believe that God is establishing us and refreshing our spirit. God is restoring our position and redeeming our time. Everything the canker worm and the locust destroyed, God is rebuilding and renewing. Through the Word, God is renewing our minds and cleansing our hearts. Despite the past and our present circumstances, right at this moment, God, *Jehovah Rapha,* is healing our wounds.

Right now God is cancelling the assignments of the enemy. Regardless of what others say about us, God is reaching out his hand beckoning for us to come unto Him and lay down

A Final Word

our burdens. I charge you to give it over to God and let him handle it and know that by doing so you are saying, "I've had enough. Satan, you are a liar. God bless you and be encouraged.

THE FIVE PILLARS

Prayer & Confession

Obeying the Voice of God

Trusting in the Lord

Walking by Faith

Grabbing Hold of your Cross

LEAVE THE LIES IN THE PAST AND

GET EXCITED ABOUT YOUR

FUTURE IN GOD!

About the Author
Minister Antoine D. Jackson

Since the beginning of time, God chose and set aside Minister Antoine D. Jackson to serve as a powerful herald of the gospel of Jesus Christ. At the young age of twelve, Jackson heard his call to the ministry. Throughout junior high, high school, and college, Jackson sought a greater understanding of his calling to the ministry. Eight years after hearing his call, he acknowledged his calling and began daily works to make full use of his anointing and appointing. He preached his first public sermon in April of 2005 at the age of twenty titled, "*Get Up Quickly; Change is Happening*". In that same year, Jackson was elevated to a deacon.

About the Author

Antoine is a gifted young man of God who has been commissioned by God to reach the lost souls of this world. Jackson was reared in the things of God, attending church with his grandmother and aunt in Detroit. Through this exposure, he discovered a love relationship with the Lord Jesus Christ and works daily to maintain its harmony. At age twelve, Antoine was baptized in the name of Jesus, and one year later was filled with the gift of the Holy Spirit with the evidence of speaking in other tongues.

He has served in numerous ministries including Praise & Worship Team Leader, Youth Director, Sunday School Teacher, Vacation Bible School Coordinator, Trustee, Chairman of the Board of Deacons and Director of Christian Education to name a few. Jackson received his Minister's License by his Pastor Waverly B. Bumbrey, Sr. of Refuge Temple Church of God In Christ. Jackson resides with his wife, Joanna, and their daughter, Madison Marie, in the surrounding metropolitan Detroit area.

About the Author

Bring Minister Antoine Jackson to your city!

For speaking engagements or to order

please email MINISTERADJACKSON@GMAIL.COM *or visit me online*

at www.AntoineJackson.org

Prayer of Salvation

I thank God for you taking the time to read this literary work. I pray that something within this work has provided you with strength, vigor, and encouragement to continue on in this race to follow Christ. Nevertheless, I understand that there may be someone reading this book who has not accepted the Lord Jesus Christ as their personal savior and I want to present to you the opportunity to do so right now. Please pray this prayer:

"Lord Jesus, come into my heart. Lord I repent and turn from all of my sins and all of my unrighteous behavior. Lord, I ask that you create in me a clean heart and renew a right spirit within me. Lord I confess with my mouth the Lord Jesus Christ and I believe in my heart that you have raised Jesus from the dead. Lord I believe that you will return to this earth to gather those who have confessed you that we may live in eternity with you in Heaven. Lord I am sorry for my actions, words, thoughts,

Prayer of Salvation

and emotions that have been contrary to your will. Please Lord, save me right now in Jesus' name! Amen!"

If you prayed that prayer to God with sincerity and in faith, my Bible tells me that you have just been saved, born again; yes, set free from the bondage of sin! I encourage you to find a Bible-based church and join it if you have not already done so. Perhaps, you may already know the Lord as your Savior and this prayer have served as a reminder of your commitment to God. I encourage you to remain faithful in the call that God has placed on your life.

TO ORDER ADDITIONAL COPIES!

Name: _____

Address: _____

City/State: _____

Zip: _____

Phone: _____

Email: _____

May we contact you about upcoming events, or when Minister Jackson visits your city?   ☐ Yes   ☐ No

How may we contact you? ☐ Email   ☐ U.S. Mail   ☐ Phone

When You've Had Enough: A Word On Breaking Free

$12.00 per book ($10 per book for orders of 10 or more)

Please visit www.AntoineJackson.org for more products.

Product Code	Quantity	Cost
WYHE	_____	_____
_____	_____	_____
_____	_____	_____
_____	_____	_____
_____	_____	_____

Make Payable and Send Orders to:
Sow Graphics & Publications
25590 West 12 Mile Rd., Ste. 204
Southfield, Michigan 48034
Purchase online at www.AntoineJackson.org or email at MinisterADJackson@Gmail.com

Made in the USA
San Bernardino, CA
18 June 2016